First published by Her Majesty's Stationery Office, 1963
This edition published by V&A Publishing, 2008
V&A Publishing
Victoria and Albert Museum
South Kensington
London SW7 2RL

Prepared by the Home Office and the Central Office of Information.

ISBN 978 1 85177 542 2

10 9 8 7 6 5 4 3 2
2012 2011 2010 2009 2008

Cover design by willwebb.co.uk

Printed in Hong Kong

V&A Publishing
Victoria and Albert Museum
South Kensington
London SW7 2RL
www.vam.ac.uk

CIVIL DEFENCE HANDBOOK No. 10

Advising the Householder on Protection against Nuclear Attack

LONDON: HER MAJESTY'S STATIONERY OFFICE

NINEPENCE NET

This is a training publication for the civil defence, the police and fire services. Its aim is to indicate to members of these services the sort of advice which would be given in a period of alert to the general public about what they might do in their homes or out-of-doors. Further advice will follow on what should be done at places of work and about children and young people in schools and establishments of further education.

CONTENTS

3

Introduction

The primary purpose of the Government's defence policy is to prevent war; but until general disarmament has been achieved and nuclear weapons brought under international control there still remains some risk of nuclear attack.

If such weapons were used in war they would cause casualties and damage on a vast scale. In areas close to the explosions most people would be killed instantly and nearly all buildings would be completely destroyed. Outside these areas the destructive effects of nuclear weapons diminish and there are precautions which could be taken to mitigate them further. Survival during and immediately after an attack would depend largely upon the actions taken by individual men and women.

This booklet tells you what you could do to protect yourself, your family and your home.

4

1 BASIC FACTS

What happens when an H-bomb explodes

The explosion of an H-bomb would cause total destruction for several miles around; the size of the area would depend on the size of the bomb and the height at which it was exploded. Outside this area survival would be possible but there would be three dangers:

HEAT   BLAST   FALL-OUT

HEAT An H-bomb explosion creates a huge white-hot fireball which lasts for about 20 seconds and gives off tremendous heat. The heat is so intense that it can kill people in the open up to several miles away. It could also burn exposed skin very much further away. Striking through unprotected windows it could set houses alight many miles away.

BLAST Blast would follow the heat waves like a hurricane. Buildings would be destroyed or severely damaged for several miles from the explosion, and there would be lighter damage for many miles beyond. There would be a further large area where, although houses suffered no structural damage, windows would be broken and there would be danger from flying glass.

FALL-OUT Fall-out is the dust that is sucked up from the ground by the explosion and made radio-active in the rising fireball. It rises high in the air and is carried down-wind, falling slowly to earth over an area which may be hundreds of miles long and tens of miles wide. Within this

5

area everything in the open would be covered with a film of radioactive fall-out dust. Fall-out would start to reach the ground in the heavily damaged areas near the explosion in about half an hour. Further away it would take longer, and about one hundred miles away the fall-out might not come down for four to six hours.

Fall-out dust gives off radiation rather like X-rays. The radiation cannot be seen or felt, heard or smelled. It can be detected only by the special instruments with which the civil defence, the police and fire services would be equipped. Exposure to radiation, that is, being too close to fall-out dust for too long, can cause sickness or death. The radiation rapidly becomes less intense with time and after two days fall-out is about one hundred times less harmful than at first . . .

. . . but even then it is still dangerous

2 PROTECTIVE MEASURES

The Fall-out Room

To protect your family against fall-out, and so far as possible against heat and blast, you would need a fall-out room, stocked and fitted out as this booklet suggests.

Choosing a Fall-out Room

The penetration of the harmful radiations from fall-out is reduced by heavy and dense materials such as brick walls, concrete or hard-packed earth. You should try to get as much of this sort of material between yourself and the fall-out as possible.

A cellar or basement gives most protection and is best for use as a fall-out room.

Otherwise—

If you live in a HOUSE...

Choose a room on the ground floor with as little outside wall as possible. The further you are from outside walls and the roof, the better the protection. A room shielded by neighbouring buildings is better than one overlooking open space.

If you live in a FLAT ...

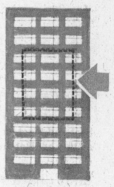

If the block of flats is of modern construction with concrete floors and is five or more storeys high, rooms in flats on the middle floors would give the best protection. If you live above or below the middle floors it would be best if you could join families living on these floors. In any case, it is important that *the top storey should* **NOT** *be used.* If the block of flats is of four storeys or less, or has wooden floor joists, the ground floor would give the best protection. If you live in the upper floors you should try to arrange to join the people living on the ground floor.

If you live in a BUNGALOW

or a SINGLE STOREY PREFABRICATED HOUSE

These dwellings give little protection. If you could arrange to join neighbours who live in more substantial buildings you should do so. If not, you should follow the instructions on pages 9 and 10 for providing a shelter "CORE" in your home.

Improving a Fall-out Room

The windows are the weak point in a fall-out room and you will not be properly protected until they have been blocked up. Do this in one or other of the following ways:

1 Put sand-bags or earth-filled containers outside the windows. If you cannot do this, block the windows from inside with bookcases, chests of drawers or other large furniture packed tightly with earth, books or other heavy material;

OR-**2** Remove the frames and put boards, planks or doors across outer and inner sills as shutters. Bolt or wire them together. Fill the intervening space with hard-packed earth or sand as the work proceeds;

OR-**3** Remove the frames and brick up the openings. Lay a double thickness of bricks if possible.

There are other things you could do to make the fall-out room more effective.

▼

Block up windows and outside doors of any hall or passage opening into the fall-out room. If the inside walls of the fall-out room are light, block up windows and outside doors of any adjoining rooms. Pieces of heavy furniture or stacks of books could be used for this. Thicken any outside walls of the fall-out room as high as possible with any heavy material—bricks, sandbags or containers filled with earth; do this *outside* the house so as not to lessen the shelter space or overload flooring joists.

Very much improved protection could be obtained by constructing a shelter "CORE". This means a smaller thick-walled shelter, built preferably inside the fall-out room itself, in which to spend the first critical hours when the radiation from fall-out would be most dangerous.

The "CORE" could take various forms, for example:

(a) a lean-to of wood, sandbagged over and resting against an inner wall;

(b) an underfloor trench;

(c) a cupboard under the stairs, sandbagged on the stairs and along the outside of the cupboard.

(See illustrations overleaf.)

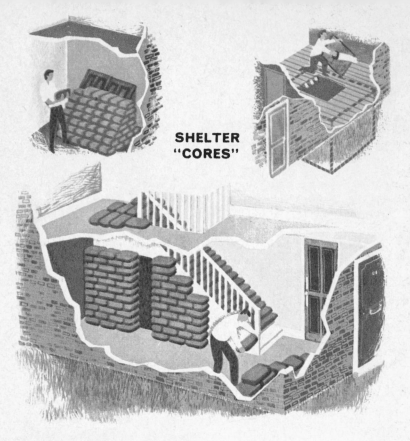

SHELTER "CORES"

Outdoor Fall-out Shelter

If it is impossible for you to prepare an indoor fall-out shelter, a trench dug outside your home would provide good protection. It should be deep enough to provide comfortable standing room and the sides should be shored up. After placing supports across the trench, cover the top with boards, metal sheets or concrete slabs, and heap earth on top. Leave a manhole-type entrance with a movable cover such as a dustbin lid. Keep a small ladder or a pair of household steps there.

3 EMERGENCY EQUIPMENT AND SUPPLIES

Equipping a Fall-out Room

Prepare your fall-out room for a stay of at least a week, but remember to leave enough space to move about in. Shelves or a cupboard will save floor space. Unless your fall-out room is large you will probably find it more convenient to divide your food stocks, and store half in the fall-out room and half within easy reach outside, say in the kitchen or larder. Remember that after there had been a warning of fall-out it would be dangerous to leave your fall-out room, except for short periods if visits to other parts of the house were necessary, for example, to obtain further supplies of food or water.

BASIC FURNITURE AND EQUIPMENT

- MATTRESSES, PILLOWS AND BLANKETS
- TABLES AND CHAIRS
- PLATES, CUPS, KNIVES, FORKS, SPOONS, TEA-POT, TIN-OPENER, BOTTLE-OPENER
- KETTLE
- SAUCEPANS
- PORTABLE STOVE AND FUEL
- PORTABLE RADIO SET AND SPARE BATTERIES
- TORCHES, BATTERIES, CANDLES, MATCHES
- FACE FLANNELS
- TOWELS
- SANITARY TOWELS
- SOAP
- TEA-TOWELS
- RUBBER OR PLASTIC GLOVES
- CLOCK
- BOOKS AND MAGAZINES
- TOYS FOR CHILDREN
- NOTEBOOK AND PENCIL
- BOX CONTAINING PERSONAL PAPERS, e.g. N.H.S. MEDICAL CARDS, SAVINGS BANK BOOKS, BIRTH AND MARRIAGE CERTIFICATES
- FIRST AID KIT (see page 24)

Food

Build up an emergency reserve of tinned or other non-perishable food needing little or no further preparation to last the whole household, and possibly one or two extra people, *for at least fourteen days.* Remember to provide for the special needs of any babies or invalids in the household; do not forget your pets.

Food is not harmed if the rays from fall-out pass through it, *but anything that had fall-out dust on it or in it would be contaminated and dangerous to eat or drink.* Wrap up all food except tinned food, and keep it in closed cabinets or cupboards.

Water

Water is more essential to life than food. After an attack the water supply from the mains may fail or it may become contaminated with fall-out.

Fill the bath and all available containers with clean water. The storage tank in the roof and the hot-water system would provide a further reserve. Keep these reserves and the storage tank in the roof covered so that fall-out cannot get into the water. Keep at least three days' supply of drinking water in sealed bottles or jars *in the fall-out room itself.* (Allow a minimum of one quart of water a day for each person.) Keep your reserves away from the light as much as you can, as water keeps better in a dark place.

12

Safeguard your water supplies

Water contaminated with fall-out should be prevented from entering the system, in order to keep the water already in it pure. This could be done by turning off the mains supply at the stopcock. Find out where the stopcock is situated and how to turn it off, so that when the time comes (see page 20) you could do this quickly.

Use water sparingly. If there is an attack, the water you have stored might have to last for as much as fourteen days.

REMEMBER, RADIATION ITSELF DOES NOT AFFECT WATER, BUT IF FALL-OUT DUST GETS INTO IT, THE WATER BECOMES DANGEROUS TO DRINK.

Sanitation

You could not rely on being able to use your W.C. There might not be enough water to flush it or the sewerage system might be damaged.

Keep the things listed below in the fall-out room or within easy reach outside the door.

LARGE RECEPTACLES WITH COVERS AND WITH IMPROVISED SEATS FOR USE AS URINAL, AND FOR EXCRETA

ASHES, DRY EARTH, OR DISINFECTANT

TOILET PAPER

CLEAN NEWSPAPERS, BROWN PAPER OR STRONG PAPER BAGS (TO WRAP UP FOOD REMAINS AND EMPTY TINS)

DUST-BIN WITH WELL FITTING LID

FOR PETS, KEEP A BOX OF EARTH OR ASHES

4 PREPARING THE HOUSE

Guard against Fire

The H-bomb's heat could not set fire to the brick or stone of a house but, striking through unprotected windows, it could set fire to the contents.

Stop the heat from entering the house

Whitewash your windows; those at the top of the building matter most. The whitewash will greatly reduce the fire risk by reflecting away much of the heat, which would have passed by the time the slower moving blast wave arrived. The blast might shatter the glass, but keeping out the heat-flash for those few seconds would prevent countless fires.

Reduce the risk of fires

Dispose of any inflammable material lying around in attics and upper storeys. Here the heat could strike most easily, but fire would be hardest to put out.

Clear away newspapers and magazines.

Get rid of boxes, firewood and inflammable rubbish from around the outside of the building.

Prepare to put out fires

Fires can be put out quite easily if tackled at once, while they are still small. If left, they spread rapidly and soon get out of control. Water is still the most effective way of dealing with fire.

Keep buckets of water on each floor

A stirrup pump or garden syringe would be very useful. If you have one, test it and make sure that it works. Keep it close to your fall-out room.

Guard against Flying Glass

Draw curtains and keep blinds lowered and closed. This will help to prevent injury from splinters of flying glass if the windows were shattered by the blast.

Other things to do

You will see later in this booklet (page 22) that after an attack you and your family might have to be moved away from where you had taken shelter. Pack necessities and any small valuables against this possibility. You would also need a change of clothing, and eating and drinking utensils; a blanket or travelling rug should be taken if possible. Pack your belongings in suitcases, travel bags or haversacks or, if you prefer, and know how to do this, in securely strapped blanket packs. Remember that you may be out in any weather and that your belongings may need protection from the rain.

KEEP YOUR LUGGAGE DOWN TO A WEIGHT YOU AND YOUR FAMILY CAN CARRY

If you have a car, make sure that the petrol tank is kept full, and that the car is ready for a journey at any time.

5 WHAT TO DO IF IT HAPPENS

WARNINGS

The warning system aims to give notice of the threat of air attack and also of fall-out. The different warnings will be as follows:

	SOUND	MEANING
RED	Siren (rising and falling note)	Imminent danger of attack
GREY	Siren (interrupted note of steady pitch) or Church bells (or, in Scotland, oral or whistle message)	Fall-out expected in an hour
BLACK	Maroon, gong or whistle sounding a Morse 'D'— dash dot dot	Imminent danger of fall-out

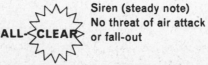

ALL-CLEAR Siren (steady note) No threat of air attack or fall-out

The Red warning (imminent danger of attack) would also be broadcast by the B.B.C.

What to do if a Warning Sounds

This is what you should do, depending on the kind of warning and where you are.

WARNING

RED
Imminent danger of attack

Take cover immediately

OUTDOORS. If you cannot reach home within four or five minutes, take cover in the nearest building.

In open country, make for any cover or, failing that, lie down in a ditch or depression in the ground, covering the exposed skin of the face and hands. If after some minutes there has been no explosion, seek the best cover you can find.

DRIVING A VEHICLE. Park off the road if possible; otherwise alongside the kerb, but not near crossroads, or in narrow streets, or where it could obstruct fire engines or civil defence vehicles. Take cover in a nearby building or in a ditch or depression if there is no building near.

VISITING. If you cannot reach home within four or five minutes, take cover where you are.

AT HOME. Turn off gas taps (including the main), cut off any fuel oil supply, disconnect electric heaters, close stoves, cover open fires with sand or earth, shut windows. Go to your fall-out room or garden shelter.

GREY
Fall-out expected in an hour

OUTDOORS. Seek safer and more comfortable surroundings before the fall-out comes down. Go home if you can get there quickly.

VISITING. Go home if you can get there quickly. Otherwise, remain under cover where you are.

AT HOME. Complete any last-minute preparations (see page 20) then return to your fall-out room.

BLACK
Imminent danger of fall-out

If you have left your fall-out room or are away from home when you hear the Black warning—

OUTDOORS. Whether in open or built-up country, immediately seek the best cover you can find.

VISITING. Take cover where you are.

AT HOME. Go immediately to your fall-out room.

17

Important

1 If there has already been a Red warning do not expose yourself needlessly to the risk of air attack. The Grey warning does not mean that another attack could not come.

2 Warnings will be cancelled by the All Clear or by word of mouth, when those sheltering from fall-out will be told what to do by wardens or police.

3 Keep the door of your fall-out room shut during warning periods. Rely for ventilation on the chimney and gaps round the door.

4 If you have been caught out-of-doors, take off your outer garments and leave them outside the fall-out room; brush your remaining clothes and wash exposed parts of the body before going to shelter. This would help to get rid of any fall-out dust you may have picked up outside.

Give shelter to anyone caught without protection near your home.

If there is No Warning

If an explosion comes without warning, the first you would know of it would be a blinding flash of heat and light lasting about 20 seconds. This would be followed after an interval by the blast wave, as thunder follows a flash of lightning.

DO NOT LOOK AT THE FLASH

Outdoors

Take cover against the *heat-flash* by flinging yourself down instantly, wherever you are.

Remain like that until the *blast wave* is over.

At home

Move instantly away from windows or open doorways and get behind anything solid. If, after the heat-flash has faded, you could get to your fall-out room in a few seconds, do so. Otherwise, remain under the best available cover till the blast wave is over.

Then put out fires (see page 20). After that, listen for warning signals of further attacks or of approaching fall-out, or for instructions from wardens or the police.

Visiting

Take cover immediately (see above) and remain there until the blast wave has passed.

Then help to put out fires (see page 20).

After that, wait for warning signals of further attacks or of approaching fall-out, or for instructions from wardens or the police.

6 WHAT TO DO IMMEDIATELY AFTER ATTACK

FIRES

As soon as the blast wave has passed, go round the house and *put out any fires before they take hold.* Turn off the gas and any fuel oil supply, if that has not been done already. Try to make sure that you are safe from any fires which have started nearby.

WATER

If the mains supply is still functioning, you could use the water for fire-fighting. But as soon as possible *turn off the water supply at the stopcock to prevent the possibility of fall-out contaminated water entering the system.*

Remember that when the stopcock has been turned off, water heaters and boilers should also be turned off, or put out. To leave them going might be dangerous.

Tie up the ball-cock in the W.C. cistern, so that clean water is not used for flushing.

These jobs are so important that they should be done despite the unknown risk from fall-out, but if you have to go outside put on gum-boots or stout shoes, a hat or headscarf, coat done up to the neck, and gloves. When you return, take these clothes off and leave them outside the fall-out room in case there is fall-out dust on them.

When you have seen to your own household, help any neighbour in need.

LISTEN FOR WARNING SIGNALS OF APPROACHING FALL-OUT

20

7 LIFE UNDER FALL-OUT CONDITIONS

THE FIRST DAYS

Once you know that there is danger from fall-out, **TAKE COVER AND DO NOT GO OUTSIDE AGAIN UNTIL YOU ARE TOLD BY WARDENS OR THE POLICE THAT IT IS SAFE TO DO SO.**

Listen for announcements on your radio. It will probably be safe to leave the fall-out room for short periods if visits to other parts of the house are necessary, for example, to obtain further supplies of food or water. *But do not go outside the house.*

This is only a general guide. The amount of fall-out would vary. It would be worst in the middle of the fall-out area, and would grow less and less towards the fringes. Everywhere, the danger from fall-out would grow less with time (see page 6).

You could not tell for yourself how bad fall-out was. This could be done only by people with special instruments, such as members of the civil defence, police and fire services. They would tell you when it was safe for you to come out in the open.

21

Very Heavy Fall-out

Where fall-out is very heavy at first, people might have to be moved to safer places as soon as they could come out of cover. You will not be able to know yourself whether you are in such an area, so listen for instructions given by wardens or police or over the radio.

Be ready to go at a
moment's notice,
**but on no account
leave home before
you are told.**

Take the suitcases or packs with necessities described on page 15. Take something to drink and enough food for 24 hours—biscuits, cheese, fruit, chocolate, glucose sweets are particularly suitable. Put your food in plastic bags, or wrap it up well. Wear warm clothing and gloves and take an overcoat.

People with cars would be asked to use them to take their families away and some neighbours if there was any room to spare.

Food

Keep food covered—*remember fall-out*. If the covering is intact the food inside is safe. There might be fall-out dust on the covering; take care this does not get on to the food. Wipe the outsides of tins and containers before opening; remove food wrapping carefully and put it straight into the dustbin outside your fall-out room. Wear rubber or plastic gloves while doing these things.

Water

Keep your reserve supplies covered—*remember fall-out*. Fall-out may contaminate the mains supply (see page 13). Remember not to use for cooking or drinking any water drawn from the mains until you are told that it is safe to do so.

Where water supplies are no longer safe, or have failed, emergency arrangements would be made for distributing water. These might take a week or more, so use your reserves of water very sparingly. Re-use water for different purposes as often as possible. After a nuclear attack, rain water would not be safe to drink, but water from wells would probably be safe.

> **Boiling does not make water fit to drink once it has been contaminated by fall-out**

HOW TO MANAGE LATER

When the danger from fall-out had lessened sufficiently, wardens or the police would tell you when you could go outside. At first this would only be for a short spell at a time to do work that had to be done.

You would be told later when you could go out for longer periods. Fall-out would still be dangerous for some time and you would still have to guard against it by not staying out-of-doors unnecessarily.

Try to avoid bringing fall-out dust in from outside. Keep a change of footwear (gumboots or stout shoes) for going out. Before coming in, take them off and wash or wipe them, soles as well.

Wipe the working surfaces in the kitchen with a damp cloth; also wipe the shelves in the larder and food cupboards. Wear rubber or plastic gloves while doing this, and afterwards wash the cloth and gloves to get rid of the dangerous fall-out dust.

Burn the contents of your dustbin and bury the ash. Burning will not get rid of the radioactivity, but it will reduce the bulk of your rubbish and help to prevent ordinary disease.

FIRST AID KIT

(a) Aspirin or codeine tablets
Adhesive plaster
Bandages, two-inch
Clean cloths
Dressings
Safety pins and scissors
Skin cream

(b) Cotton wool
Salt, household, one half-pound
Soda, bicarbonate (Baking Powder), four-ounce
packet.
Bowls, various sizes, three
Hot-water bottles and covers
Teaspoons
Vaseline

(c) Talcum powder
Paper handkerchiefs
Methylated or surgical spirit

(d) Clean cotton rags in plastic bags
Disinfectant
Packet of strong sewing needles
Reel of white cotton